STEPS TO TAKE WHEN BUYING PROPERTY IN MEXICO

THIS ARTICLE IS FROM A MODIFIED CHAPTER FROM THE BOOK "HOW TO BUY REAL ESTATE IN MEXICO" AND IT EXAMINES AN EIGHT-STEP PROCESS FOR BUYING REAL ESTATE IN MEXICO. THE CONTRACTS USED IN REAL ESTATE TRANSACTIONS IN MEXICO ARE EXAMINED IN DETAIL. THESE CONTRACTS INCLUDE THE OFFER AND ACCEPTANCE, PROMISSORY AGREEMENTS, AND VARIOUS FORMS OF A SALES AGREEMENT. THE STEPS ARE PRESENTED IN SEQUENCE. THE SECTIONS EXPLAINING EACH STEP ADDRESS THE NECESSARY PROCEDURES AND DESCRIBE THE PEOPLE INVOLVED.

I0494186

INTRODUCTION

Once a prospective buyer decides on a piece of property in Mexico, the next step is to determine whether the seller has legal title. Although this seems to be a logical and natural precaution, there have been instances in which foreigners thought they had acquired real estate only to find out later that the seller was unable to transfer title because he didn't own the land.

This chapter will examine some of the legal restrictions confronted by foreigners when buying real estate in Mexico, as well as the necessity of a real estate trust. Once the decision is made to acquire property in Mexico there are some basic considerations to be examined. The following section examines some of the procedures involved in property ownership in the restricted zone.

The first thing a buyer must consider is whether the seller of the property has legal title to the property, and, if so, whether the property can be legally transferred. Before a buyer can answer these questions, he must consider how much he knows about the applicable laws and regulations and whether he is capable of obtaining this information on his own. He may be better off seeking help and advice of a Mexican attorney.

A buyer must always remember that he is not in the United States. The rules are not the same! It is easy to assume this, especially when dealing with American real estate agents, sellers, etc. throughout the transaction. The Mexican legal system is not the same as its American equivalent.

This is not to say that in Mexico real estate transactions are totally different or more complicated than those in the U.S. are, but common sense should be exercised. When buying property in Mexico, or any foreign country, a buyer should take the same precautions he would take when buying the same property in the United States. In the United States this procedure is fairly straightforward since real estate transactions are legally regulated. Consequently, in the United States real estate brokers and agents generally handle much of the transaction. Since no such regulations exist in Mexico, a buyer must know who the players are in any real estate transaction, and who to turn to for help and assistance when necessary.

The worst a buyer can do is remain ignorant to the law and procedures involved in real estate transactions in Mexico. Typically the seller is already somewhat knowledgeable in these areas since he has been through a real estate transaction at lease once before in Mexico. However, the buyer should not depend on the seller for information or advice because he has no way of knowing if it is correct. The buyer should always seek the advice of a Mexican attorney to make sure that she clearly understands what is taken place.

This working article is hosted by Law Mexico Publishing and may not be commercially reproduced without the permission of the copyright holder. http://lawmexico.com/publications.htm Copyright 2009 Dennis John Peyton.

REAL ESTATE CONTRACTS

The most common types of real estate contracts in Mexico are the following:

- Offer and acceptance *(oferta)*
- Promissory agreement (*contrato de promesa*)
- Real estate trust agreement *(contrato de fideicomiso)*
- Purchase-sales agreement *(contrato de compraventa)*
- Purchase-sales agreement with reservation of title *(contrato de compraventa con reserva de dominio)*
- Assignment of real estate trusts rights (*contrato de cesion de derechos fideicomisarios*)

Most real estate transactions will have at least two contracts:

- **Offer and acceptance and/or a promissory agreement**: a preliminary agreement containing only the basic information. It is not the instrument by which title to the property is transferred to the buyer.
- **Purchase sales agreement**: the agreement by which title transfers to the buyer. It may take different forms: a reserve title agreement, or a real estate trust agreement.

The Civil Code defines an agreement *(convenio)* as an accord *(acuerdo)* between two or more persons to create, transfer, modify or extinguish obligations. More specifically, the Civil Code defines contracts as agreements that produce or transfer obligations and rights.

LEGAL REQUIREMENTS

In order for contracts to legally exist the following requirements must exist:

- Consent: this is the acceptance or approval of what is agreed to in the contract by buyer and the seller.
- A legal object which is subject-matter of the contract: this refers to the property which must be property that can be sold.

A contract may be judged invalid for any of the following reasons:

- One or both of the parties lacks legal capacity to contract.
- Defects (*vicios*) of consent: this refers to case when one or both of the parties did not properly consent to enter into the agreement due to violence, error, or fraud;
- The contract's object, motive or purpose *(fin)* is illegal;
- The consent given by one or both of the parties is not expressed in the form prescribed by law.

As a general rule, real estate contracts must be recorded before a public notary and, to be binding before third parties, filed with the public registry.

There are three contracts normally involved in a real estate transaction in the restricted zone:

- Offer to Purchase
- Promissory Agreement
- Trust Agreement or Deed to the property.

Cases involving property outside of the restricted zone may not require a promissory agreement because there usually is not a delay in getting the deed *(escrituras públicas)* to the

This working article is hosted by Law Mexico Publishing and may not be commercially reproduced without the permission of the copyright holder. http://lawmexico.com/publications.htm Copyright 2009 Dennis John Peyton.

property transferred to the buyer. However, in any transaction, outside or within the restricted zone, if the buyer is making payments over an extended period of time, or for any reason the actual transference of title is delayed for more than a few weeks a promissory agreement should be used.

STEP ONE: OFFER AND ACCEPTANCE

Most often the first document a potential buyer sees in a real estate transaction in Mexico is an Offer to Purchase Contract. The contract takes many different forms in Mexico, and has many different names. Some of the most common names given to this contract are:

➤ Offer and Acceptance
➤ Offer to Purchase
➤ Offer to Purchase and Earnest Money Deposit
➤ Earnest Money Deposit

From a legal standpoint, an offer is any proposition which one person makes to another to enter into a contract under certain conditions. The law states that anyone who proposes the execution of a contract to another person, fixing a time for its acceptance, is bound by his offer until the expiration of the time period proposed.

The law recognizes "express" or "tacit" consent when determining when an offer has been accepted. The consent is "expressly" given when it is given verbally, in writing or by unequivocal signs. "Tacit" consent is given when the facts or acts involved in the transaction warrant the presumption of consent, except when by law or agreement the consent must be "expressly" given.

In other words, the fact that an offer and an acceptance were not made in writing does not mean that the parties did not consent to the terms of the sale. This can result in confusion regarding the terms and conditions agreed to by the buyer and the seller. For this reason, a buyer must **make sure both the offer and acceptance are made in writing**.

By writing out the offer and acceptance the parties are more likely to address the main points of the transaction and avoid confusion when it comes time to sign contracts. At this stage in the transaction, a buyer is only proposing that a sales contract or promissory agreement be executed. Not all of the details of the transaction will be addressed; they will be dealt with in the sales contract or promissory agreement, once more detailed information is made available and an investigation of the title to the property is done.

There have been cases where a potential buyer has had his offer accepted by the seller and has given an earnest money deposit to the seller's real estate agent. He finds out later, however, when the contract is drawn up, that there are other conditions of which he is unaware and is unwilling to accept. This is especially true in transactions involving buyers who have no knowledge of how real estate transactions are carried out in Mexico.

The seller or his real estate agent is not necessarily trying to hide anything, but it is often assumed that the buyer knows how the transaction is to be carried out. The real estate agent may not even know what the sales contract or promissory agreement will contain because they are drafted in Spanish by the company's lawyers. To be safe, a buyer must insist that he will not fully consent to the purchase until he is able to review the final agreement in English and verify that the Spanish version contains the same information. The buyer should always request that all agreements be done in both English and Spanish. Both version should be then be reviewed by a Mexican attorney.

This working article is hosted by Law Mexico Publishing and may not be commercially reproduced without the permission of the copyright holder. http://lawmexico.com/publications.htm Copyright 2009 Dennis John Peyton.

If possible, the buyer should request that the property be taken off the market for two weeks so that his lawyer has time to draft the final agreement. For this short amount of time, the seller shouldn't require an earnest money deposit. If he does, it should be refundable. If the seller requires a non-refundable earnest money deposit, the buyer should be sure it is not more than he is willing to lose. Whatever the case may be, everything should be in writing. A buyer must not take the real estate agent's word that his money will be refunded. He must insist that it be in writing and without any conditions. Although most real estate agents can be trusted it is always better to put everything in writing.

HOW TO EXECUTE

Normally the real estate company will have either an Offer To Purchase and Deposit Receipt form for the buyer to fill out, or they will have a boilerplate in their computer that can be modified for each offer. Either the real estate agent or the buyer's attorney will hold earnest money deposits. When small sums of money are involved a real estate agent can hold the deposit. The buyer should have an attorney set up a trust account to hold the deposit when large sums of money are involved. Since attorneys are licensed they are held much more accountable than real estate agents in relations with there clients. The offer must clearly indicate who received the earnest money. It will need to be clear in case the buyer wants a refund.

A prospective buyer must carefully read and clearly understand the offer before signing it, particularly when he has a new real estate agent. If there is something the buyer does not understand, he should have it removed or rewritten. A buyer must not accept the inclusion of anything he does not clearly understand, even if the real estate agent insists that it must be included by law. Common sense should dictate what is or is not included in an agreement. As long as the provisions do not entail breaking the law, any special provisions may be included in the offer or acceptance.

Most of the well-established real estate companies are experienced enough to avoid the pitfalls associated with making offers. By including certain provisions, "escape clauses," in the written offer, one is able to protect the buyer's interests by not releasing any earnest money deposited with them until a written acceptance and, if necessary, a promissory agreement are signed, at which time such deposits become non-refundable.

More often than not the offer to purchase will include provisions for an earnest money deposit. A buyer should take care to clearly understand the provisions regarding the refund of the deposited money. He must make it clear that he wants a written guarantee that his money will be refunded if either a promissory agreement or a final sales agreement isn't executed in a certain amount of time.

An earnest money deposit is typically a deposit made by the buyer to evidence good faith that he is serious about going ahead with the transaction. This is necessary in order for the seller to avoid having his property tied up and possibly miss a sale. For this reason, the seller may require that the money deposited not be refundable.

A foreign buyer may not be aware of exactly what steps need to be taken in a Mexican real estate transaction and therefore may require time to consult with an attorney before agreeing to the exact sales conditions. This is expected and should be made clear from the beginning. In most cases, the parties should agree to include only the most basic conditions in the offer, and should agree to a term of one or two weeks to have the final contracts drawn up. If during this period, the buyer should choose not to buy the property, his deposit should be refunded.

This working article is hosted by Law Mexico Publishing and may not be commercially reproduced without the permission of the copyright holder. http://lawmexico.com/publications.htm Copyright 2009 Dennis John Peyton.

A buyer should not commit to the purchase of the property before having a clear idea of the variables that may affect the transaction. There is always something that the parties didn't consider or didn't write into the offer. This can cause problems and possibly the loss of the deposit. Therefore, if possible, the buyer should insist that he be given a reasonable period of time to investigate the property and consult an attorney before the earnest money deposit becomes non-refundable.

The property will stay on the market until the buyer has received a written acceptance of his offer. The terms and conditions of the buyer's offer do not bind the seller until the seller accepts the offer. However, such acceptance can be considered provisional as long as a promissory agreement has not been executed. Consequently, if the transaction will not be completed in more than a few days, it is in the interests of both the buyer and the seller to execute the promissory agreement as soon as possible once acceptance is received.

In smaller real estate transactions that involve a single parcel or a single family home, the importance of the offer is minimal, and is often reduced to a mere formality by which the real estate agent is able to take the property off the market. However, even if the offer is verbal, a buyer should include the condition that he must see the sales contract or promissory agreement before his offer is final.

Unless the buyer has total confidence in his agent's capabilities, he should have an attorney review the documents before signing them. Most real estate agents have little or no training or education in Mexican real estate transactions. Many also speak little or no Spanish. Therefore it is always a good idea to get an educated opinion before signing any documents.

Once there is a **written** acceptance to the offer, the buyer's attorney should draw up the sales contract or promissory agreement. Since this agreement is the single most important document the buyer will execute with the seller, and the agreement's contents will determine the terms and conditions of the transaction, the buyer should insist that his attorney assume this responsibility.

The real estate company usually includes a fee in the **"closing costs"** to cover the costs of having the sales contract or promissory agreement drawn up. If this is the case, the buyer can have that amount deducted from the closing costs and hire his own attorney. Often he will pay the same amount, or a little more to hire his own attorney, but, by doing so, he has someone responsible and knowledgeable to represent his interests.

WHEN AND HOW LONG AN OFFER IS VALID

The law recognizes express or tacit consent when determining when an offer has been given and accepted. The consent is expressly given when it is given verbally, in writing or by unequivocal signs. Tacit consent is given when the facts or acts involved in the transaction warrant the presumption of consent, except when by law or agreement the consent must be expressly given. The law states that anyone who proposes the execution of a contract to another person, fixing a time for its acceptance, is bound by his offer until the expiration of the time proposed.

The law also includes other provisions regarding the period of time an offer is binding as follows:

1. When the offer is made to a person present, or by telephone, without fixing a time for acceptance, the person making the offer, the "offerer," must honor the offer only if it is accepted immediately.

This working article is hosted by Law Mexico Publishing and may not be commercially reproduced without the permission of the copyright holder. http://lawmexico.com/publications.htm Copyright 2009 Dennis John Peyton.

2. When the offer is made without a time limit to a person not present, the offerer is bound for three days, plus the time necessary for the mail to be sent to that person and returned to the offerer.

3. The contract is formed at the moment the offerer receives the acceptance of the offer, being bound until then as provided above.

4. The offer, as well as the acceptance, is considered as not made, if it is withdrawn before the other party receives the offer or the acceptance.

5. If at the time of acceptance the offerer has died, without the knowledge of the acceptor, the heirs of the offerer are bound to fulfill the contract.

6. The offerer does not have to honor his offer if the acceptance is not in the exact terms offered; if it involves any modification, it is considered as a new offer subject to the same conditions for acceptance as the original offer.

7. An offer and acceptance by telegraph are effective, if the parties had previously agreed in writing to contract in this manner, and if the originals of the respective telegrams contain the signatures of the parties.

Note that, under the provisions of number 6 above, a counter-offer is legally considered as a new offer. As such, the role of the offerer and acceptor are reversed. This allows the buyer, upon receiving a counter-offer from the seller, the right to withdraw from the transaction completely. In other words, the buyer does not have to honor his first offer. This is very important, especially in complicated real estate transactions with many rounds of negotiations.

ESCROW AND EARNEST MONEY DEPOSITS

Because of the similarities in real estate transactions in general, it is easy to assume that the basic terms and principles with which a buyer is familiar in the US also hold true in Mexico. This assumption becomes easier to make when US real estate terminology is adopted, and much of the paperwork is similar, if not exactly the same, as that used in the US. Without a doubt, there are many aspects of Mexican real estate transactions that are identical to procedures carried out in the United States, but a buyer is much better off to assume nothing.

What is escrow? The Encyclopedic Dictionary of Business Law defines escrow as follows:

> In business or in real property transactions, the delivery of personal property, usually money, to a third person to be held by him until a certain condition agreed upon in advance is met. Upon the occurrence of that event, the escrow property is to be delivered to the party as provided for in the original agreement.

In the United States, an escrow company or a person legally empowered to act as an escrow agent will act in this capacity. In some states, attorneys handle escrow and the activity is commonly known as "settlement." In any case, the individual or company who carries out the escrow or settlement procedures is licensed and empowered by law to do so, and is legally responsible to see that the agreed upon conditions are met before any funds are released.

The word "escrow" is not easily translated into Spanish. One term that is often used is "*arras*." *Arras* is roughly translated as follows: the deposit of a sum of money or property that one contracting party makes with the other contracting party upon the execution of a contract for a specific purpose. Normally the use of *arras* is intended to assure the performance and fulfillment of the terms and conditions of the contract in question.

There is a significant difference between escrow and *arras*, in that, by definition, escrow always involves the services of a third party, which is not the case with *arras*.

This working article is hosted by Law Mexico Publishing and may not be commercially reproduced without the permission of the copyright holder. http://lawmexico.com/publications.htm Copyright 2009 Dennis John Peyton.

The participation of a third party in escrow services in Mexico presents some very serious problems. First of all, when an individual or company offers escrow service, it is assumed that this service is being offered to the public in general. In other words, the individual or company is offering to hold money, normally for their clients or for the public in general, until certain contractual conditions are met, at which time such funds are to be released as payment or fulfillment of the contractual obligations in question.

The use of the word "escrow" or "escrow company" in any real estate transaction in Mexico is deceiving. Any service in Mexico that claims to be anything like an escrow company, without any affiliation to a Mexican bank or credit institution, is suspect.

Escrow services usually refer to legally regulated and authorized companies, or licensed individuals. Real estate "brokers" are not licensed in Mexico and escrow companies do not exist in Mexico. It is possible, however, to establish an escrow company in Mexico, because nowhere in Mexican Law is the **trust**, or **escrow** account, prohibited.

The choice of the word "trust" in this case is interesting and accurate. If it were possible to translate the word "escrow" with all its baggage and depth of meaning, the word in Spanish would be "*fideicomiso*." Two of the largest banks in Mexico, which were consulted on this subject, agreed with this translation.

An escrow account or escrow service must be handled through a "*fideicomiso*" if it is to be similar to those in the US. A "*fideicomiso*" can only be administered by a credit institution in Mexico.

The reason for this is simple. Credit institutions and Mexican banks are legally regulated and authorized to receive and solicit funds from the public. They also have the fiduciary obligations that come with the job, and therefore have the financial backing to guarantee their work, as well as protect the public interest.

Why are escrow services regulated in the U.S.? If just anyone could set up an escrow company, without any regulations or licensing, such services would probably not exist. If they did exist, not many people would use them. They would not inspire much confidence.

Given the nature of the activities carried out by "escrow services" only banks and legally established credit institutions may act as escrow companies in Mexico. There is no alternative. If someone is offering escrow services he is probably doing so because he does not understand what the word escrow means, or because it is a convenient way to simulate real estate transactions from the US and make a foreign buyer more comfortable with the deal.

The best alternative is to use an attorney's client trust account. By doing so, the parties are dealing with a licensed professional regulated by the government. This is preferable to making deposits with unlicensed real estate agents who typically do not set-up a separate account for deposits.

STEP TWO: PROMISSORY AGREEMENT

It is recommended that a promissory agreement *(contrato de promesa)* be executed as soon as both parties have agreed to the basic conditions for the purchase of the property. **In transactions outside of the restricted zone, this contract is not necessary if both parties are ready to execute the sales contract immediately**. However, when there is any delay between the execution of the offer and acceptance and the execution of the final notarized sales agreement, it is always better to enter into a promissory agreement.

This working article is hosted by Law Mexico Publishing and may not be commercially reproduced without the permission of the copyright holder. http://lawmexico.com/publications.htm Copyright 2009 Dennis John Peyton.

The three most common forms of this agreement in real estate transactions are:

➢ Promise to execute a sale;
➢ Promise to execute a real estate trust;
➢ Promise to execute an assignment of the beneficial rights of a real estate trust.

The first is used most often in transactions outside of the restricted zone, or for nonresidential properties within the restricted zone. The second and third are commonly used in transactions involving properties in the restricted zone. In fact, until the December 1993 Foreign Investment Law, they were the only alternatives in the restricted zone.

In the restricted zone foreigners may not hold direct title to property and it takes time to get the necessary permits and documentation to transfer title to a real estate trust. The purpose of such a promissory agreement is to allow the parties a sufficient amount of time to obtain the necessary documents required to execute the transaction. It also allows time to fix the basic terms and conditions for sale of the property in a legally binding agreement.

With the recent changes which are in effect for 1997, trust permits are now valid for an unlimited period of time. These changes have made it easier for the buyer to obtain a trust permit quickly without having to worry about it expiring before the trust can be set-up. For this reason the buyer should always insist that a trust permit be applied for before entering into a long term commitment under a promissory agreement.

When a buyer is unable to complete a real estate transaction immediately upon coming to an understanding with the seller on the basic conditions for the sale, the execution of a promissory agreement is imperative. Once the buyer submits a written offer to buy the property, and receives a written acceptance for such an offer, a promissory agreement should be executed.

Under normal circumstances, a real estate company is involved in the transaction, and they will have the necessary documents to complete the offer and acceptance. If a buyer is purchasing property directly from the owner, it is very likely that this first step of offer and acceptance will be omitted. Traditionally, Mexicans execute these transactions by a mere handshake.

The promissory agreement, on the other hand, should never be omitted, regardless of whether the transaction is being handled by a real estate company or directly with the owner of the property. Although the offer to purchase and its acceptance have legal effects, this in itself does not legally bind the parties to carry out the sale of the property in question.

For example, Mr. Jones makes a written offer to buy a certain piece of property from Mr. Caballero, and Mr. Caballero, in turn, gives Mr. Jones a written acceptance of that offer. Mr. Caballero decides later not to sell the property to Mr. Jones; Mr. Caballero may be liable for any damages caused to Mr. Jones by his withdrawing from the transaction. Nevertheless, Mr. Jones has to take legal action to recover any such damages, which involves a considerable amount of time and effort, and the outcome may not be to his total satisfaction.

To avoid these situations, Mexican Law permits the use of preparatory or preliminary agreements known as promissory agreements *(contrato de promesa)*.

Under the legal provisions for a promissory agreement, the law specifies that the parties to an agreement may assume the **obligation to execute a future agreement**. In other words, one or both of the parties to the promissory agreement promise to execute another agreement at some specific time in the future if certain terms and conditions are met. In real estate transactions involving foreigners, the agreement that the parties promise to execute is a real estate trust agreement or sales agreement depending upon where the property is located.

This working article is hosted by Law Mexico Publishing and may not be commercially reproduced without the permission of the copyright holder. http://lawmexico.com/publications.htm Copyright 2009 Dennis John Peyton.

For example, the conditions might be as follows: Mr. Caballero promises to execute a real estate trust agreement in order to sell Mr. Jones his property in Loreto for $10,000, provided that a real estate trust can be established in order for Mr. Jones to obtain beneficial rights. In turn, Mr. Jones promises to execute the same agreement and pay Mr. Caballero the amount specified, provided that the title to the property can be legally transferred to the real estate trust free and clear.

The promissory agreement is similar to a **letter of intent** in that the parties intend to execute a contract sometime in the future, and that it is their intent to carry out a specific action as a condition to reaching some mutual point where the contract can be executed.

A promissory agreement under Mexican Law is different from a letter of intent, or similar agreements in the United States, because the parties to the promissory agreement are bound by its terms to execute an agreement in the future. If the promissor should refuse to execute the agreement as promised, a judge may sign and execute the agreement for him by default. In other words, if a buyer has a promissory agreement with a seller to have some real estate held in trust, and the seller decides not to go through with the deal, the buyer can get a judgment and have the judge execute the necessary documents to have the property legally transferred to the trust without the intervention of the seller.

If a promissory agreement wasn't used the buyers position is much weaker in the event that the seller does not go through with the transaction. No one wants to get into a legal battle, but, when there is no other choice, it is always best to have all the elements of the transaction clearly defined in a written agreement. This is precisely what the buyer gets when a promissory agreement is used.

LEGAL REQUIREMENTS FOR A PROMISSORY AGREEMENT

In order for a promissory agreement to be valid it must meet the following requirements:

➢ The agreement must be in writing.
➢ The parties to the agreement must have legal capacity to contract.
➢ The agreement must include the principle characteristics of the future agreement.
➢ The future agreement must be executed within a specific term.

The parties to any contract must have **legal capacity** to contract. This means that the parties are adults, which in Mexico means 18 years or older, and the parties must have full use and control of their mental faculties.

Foreigners no longer need special visas in order to contract in Mexico. In June of 1990 legislative reforms were passed enabling foreigners to acquire real estate, as well as the rights associated with real estate, without requiring a special visa.

The content of the promissory agreement must include **the basic elements of the future agreement**. This means that the agreement includes the names of the parties, the name of the bank that will act as the trustee, and the price or consideration involved in the transaction. To make sure all bases are covered, a buyer can attach a draft of the future agreement to the promissory agreement. It becomes an exhibit to the contract. That way there is no doubt as to what the basic elements of the future agreement are.

Finally, the contract is limited to a **specific term**. It is best to be precise as to the amount of time the parties have to execute the agreement. For example, the promissory agreement may include a term of one year from the date of its signing for the execution of the final agreement.

This working article is hosted by Law Mexico Publishing and may not be commercially reproduced without the permission of the copyright holder. http://lawmexico.com/publications.htm Copyright 2009 Dennis John Peyton.

In most real estate transactions in Mexico, the real estate company or agent is acting on behalf of the seller. Often they use contracts drawn up by attorneys hired by the seller. Worse yet, some use contracts that were "acquired" from another company and are supposedly good for any transaction. As a result, the agreements entirely favor the seller, or they are flawed to such a degree that if they are ever subject to litigation, the agreements are useless.

Larger developments that have their own sales agents, as well as some of the well-established real estate companies, provide the buyer with promissory agreements and suggest that he review it with his attorney. These agreements can be very complicated because of all the different factors that must be considered, such as master trusts, land held under condominium regulations, and association fees. They are not drawn up to take advantage of the buyer but they are also not written with the buyer's interests in mind.

After the promissory agreement is signed and executed the seller should contact a bank selected by the buyer to start the initial trust application. Since the seller hold title to the property he must consent to having the property transferred to the trust. After this has been done, the buyer is usually responsible for making sure the bank obtains authorization from the Foreign Relations Ministry to set-up a real estate trust.

If the seller has not already done so, the buyer is also responsible for obtaining, or at least paying for, an official appraisal, a certificate of no encumbrances, and a certificate of no tax debt for the property. None of these responsibilities are set by law and the buyer should first request that the seller provide these documents. Usually the buyer assumes such responsibilities in a sellers market. This is very often the case in tourist developments.

Once these documents are obtained, they must be presented to a public notary. At this point the buyer should verify that the notary has all the necessary documents to complete the transaction and subsequently file it at the public registry. If everything is in order, the notary will work with the bank and the buyer's attorney to have the trust documents drawn up and executed at the notary's office.

If a buyer decides to have his real estate agent handle these procedures, he should know how much it will cost beforehand. Very often these services are included in the "closing costs" which the buyer is solely responsible for, and in many cases at a fee higher than an attorney will charge. If a buyer is going to pay the same or more for these services, it is in his interest to hire an attorney who will usually finish the process faster while ensuring that the procedures are being carried out correctly.

The buyer should always confirm who the real estate agent is representing. If the agent is being paid a commission from the seller then he or she is acting as the seller's agent. This is most often the case. There are some real estate agents who represent only buyers but they are few and far between. Therefore it is preferable that the buyer retain a Mexican attorney to make sure that his interests are really represented and the best possible price for the property is negotiated.

Certain words and phrases are often misused in real estate transactions in Mexico, many times at the buyer's expense. A buyer should never accept such broad terms as "closing costs" in any agreement. A buyer should always get a detailed list of what will be included in so called "closing costs" as well as any other blanket descriptions used in contracts to cover several costs or expenses. If there is no legal reason for the buyer to pay a certain cost or expense a request should be made to have the seller pay for it. There is no reason for a buyer to be shy in these matters. Very often the only reason the buyer is stuck with certain cost and expenses is because nothing was ever said to the contrary. Speak and ye shall be heard. If the buyer is uncomfortable

This working article is hosted by Law Mexico Publishing and may not be commercially reproduced without the permission of the copyright holder. http://lawmexico.com/publications.htm Copyright 2009 Dennis John Peyton.

or unable to confront the real estate agent or seller on these matters, an attorney should be hired to do so.

SPECIAL CONSIDERATIONS

It is important to understand the purpose of a promissory agreement so as to avoid misusing it and possibly violating the law. A foreign buyer must consider the following if he is thinking about using a promissory agreement.

Is it really an agreement to execute a contract in the future? There have been many cases where the parties choose to use a promissory agreement simply to avoid complying with the law. They call it a promissory agreement, but in reality it's a sales agreement. This is usually done to avoid paying taxes or to gain possession of property in the restricted zone without using a real estate trust.

The promissory agreement should not be used instead of the final agreement. A promissory agreement is only used to bind the parties to the execution of an agreement in the future because they are unable to execute that final agreement immediately.

There are many reasons why the buyer and the seller may not be able to execute the final agreement right away. The most common reason is the property has to be put into a real estate trust or is being held in a real estate trust. Either a trust must be established, which requires the intervention of a bank and a permit from the government, or the rights to the trust must be assigned over to the buyer, which also requires the intervention of a bank and a notification to the government. In both cases it is impossible to establish the trust or assign the beneficial rights in the trust immediately.

Every real estate transaction has some tax consequences. Therefore, it is important to determine exactly when the transaction takes place in order to avoid fines and late tax interest payments. For example, if the tax authorities determine that the sale of the property took place at the time the parties signed a promissory agreement, and not two years later when the real estate trust was established, the parties to the contract are responsible for two years of fines and interest payments. These can be very substantial. If it were determined that the parties intentionally avoided paying their taxes, criminal actions could also be taken against them.

A buyer can avoid these problems if the following rules are followed when deciding if a promissory agreement is the right agreement for the transaction.

A buyer must ensure that the promissory agreement is not a sale in disguise. There are two court decisions that deal with this problem:

➢ **Rule One:** If the promissory agreement does not contain the exclusive obligation to do something (such as execute another agreement), or if the property is delivered and the price is paid in whole or in part, the agreement is considered a sales agreement. This is regardless of what the parties to the contract call it.

➢ **Rule Two:** A promissory agreement is valid when the purpose of the contract is to execute an agreement in the future; in other words, the parties to the contract must again give their consent to something other than what they consented to in the promissory agreement.

Some concrete examples will help to explain when a promissory agreement is really a sales agreement.

This working article is hosted by Law Mexico Publishing and may not be commercially reproduced without the permission of the copyright holder. http://lawmexico.com/publications.htm Copyright 2009 Dennis John Peyton.

EXAMPLES

Example 1: Purchase of property in the restricted zone: Mr. Gonzalez has some beachfront property in the restricted zone that Mr. Leo wants to purchase. The parties come to an agreement on the price and are ready to complete the transaction. But, Mr. Leo is a foreigner, and the property is in the restricted zone, so they must obtain a trust permit. Additionally, Mr. Leo will need more time to make full payment and since this will take about four to six weeks, they decide to execute a promissory agreement so that Mr. Gonzalez can receive most of the purchase price right away. Mr. Leo agrees to do this only if he is given legal possession of the property. They have a promissory agreement drawn up stipulating these conditions.

Example 2: Assignment of beneficial trust rights: Mr. Smith owns a beach front home in Baja California which is held in a real estate trust. Mr. Jones offers to buy the home but can only do so if Mr. Smith agrees to receive half the money upon signing the promissory agreement, and the other half within two years. They agree and have the promissory agreement drawn up. Mr. Smith receives payment and Mr. Jones takes possession of the property.

Example 3: Purchase of property outside of the restricted zone: Mr. Smith owns a home in Guadalajara, which is not held in a real estate trust because it is not in the restricted zone. Mr. Jones offers to buy the home but can only do so if Mr. Smith agrees to receive half the money upon signing the promissory agreement and the other half within two years. They agree and have the promissory agreement drawn up. Mr. Smith receives payment and Mr. Jones takes possession of the property.

EXPLANATION AND SOLUTIONS

Example 1: Purchase of property in the restricted zone. In example 1 above, Mr. Gonzalez is paid in full and Mr. Leo takes possession of the property. This violates Rule Number One above because the property was delivered and the price was paid in full or in part. Additionally, they have also broken Rule Number Two because legally the parties have already consented to the sale of the property. Therefore, there is nothing else for them to consent to regarding a future sale: Mr. Gonzalez has already delivered the property and Mr. Leo has already paid the purchase price.

The easiest solution to this problem is not to pay the purchase price or take delivery of the property until the government issues the trust permit. Often, the parties to the agreement need some assurance that the transaction will be completed so that plans can be made, or so the buyer can warrant paying to obtain a trust permit and establishing the trust.

If the parties feel that payment of the purchase price right away is indispensable, the law allows a deposit clause to be included in the promissory agreement *(depósito)* instead of making a payment. The money paid by the buyer is considered temporarily deposited with the seller and is to be returned to the buyer as agreed to by the parties. Once the trust permit is obtained, the parties then rescind the deposit agreement and apply the money to the payment of the sales price.

If it is not necessary to take delivery of the property when the promissory agreement is executed, then it is best that delivery be taken upon execution of the trust agreement. Normally, it is not necessary for the buyer to take legal possession of the property before the trust agreement is signed. If the seller does not comply with the promissory agreement a judge may do so for him by default.

However, if possession must be taken by the buyer before they trust permit is issued or before the final sales agreement is entered into, the seller should enter into a bailment *(comodato)* or a lease agreement with the buyer. The reason for this is without some kind of an agreement to the

This working article is hosted by Law Mexico Publishing and may not be commercially reproduced without the permission of the copyright holder. http://lawmexico.com/publications.htm Copyright 2009 Dennis John Peyton.

contrary, it is assumed that the buyer would be taking ownership of the property. This would be in violation of article 27 of the Mexican Constitution.

A bailment can be defined as the rightful possession of property by one who is not their owner. The bailee (the person holding the property) by virtue of his or her possession, owes a duty of care to the bailor (the owner of the property). In other words, the bailee is responsible for taking care of the property while it is in his or her possession.

In a bailment agreement the seller is allowing the buyer the use of the property free of charge on the condition that the property will be returned to the seller under certain conditions at some time in the future. The bailment would be in effect until the title of the property can be conveyed to the buyer legally. At that time the contract could be rescinded and the final sales agreement could be executed. Since the buyer is only legally entitled to use the property under the bailment, he is not considered the owner, and, therefore, there is no violation to the Constitution.

There has been somewhat of a debate among lawyers in Mexico regarding the use of a bailment agreement for real estate since this type of agreement is usually used for personal or moveable property. However, more recently it has been accepted that its use with real estate is legal.

The other alternative for taking possession of the property is through a lease. With a lease the buyer can make rent payments that can be deducted later form the sales price.

Example 2: Assignment of beneficial trust rights. In example two above, the property is held in a real estate trust, and the seller does not legally own the property. What he does own are the beneficial rights to the real estate trust. Therefore, the seller is selling his rights in the trust rather than the real property itself. Although the outcome is the same as a real estate sale, the procedure is somewhat different.

When selling property that is held in trust, a seller is actually **assigning** his right in the trust to the buyer. Therefore, the promissory agreement is a **promise to assign trust rights**, and the final agreement is an **assignment of trust rights**.

In an assignment of trust rights, the buyer assumes the rights and obligations to the bank/trustee and to the Mexican government that the seller used to have in relation to the property. This means that the buyer must abide by the same terms and conditions that applied to the seller. Such terms and conditions are found in three sources:

➢ The trust permit issued by the Ministry of Foreign Affairs.
➢ The trust agreement which designates the bank as trustee and the buyer as the beneficiary.
➢ Applicable Mexican Law.

All of the buyer's rights are subject to the conditions in the trust permit, because without the trust permit the trust could not be established. Therefore, in order to assign the rights one has in a real estate trust, one must first make sure that the provisions of the trust permit or the trust agreement are not being violated by the assignment.

Currently, the Ministry of Foreign Affairs requires that the bank notify them before an assignment of trust rights is carried out. This is because each new beneficiary must agree to the inclusion of the Calvo clause in the trust agreement. Any assignment of trust rights executed without first notifying the Ministry of Foreign Affairs is in violation of the trust permit and, therefore, against the law.

This working article is hosted by Law Mexico Publishing and may not be commercially reproduced without the permission of the copyright holder. http://lawmexico.com/publications.htm Copyright 2009 Dennis John Peyton.

The trust agreements also require the trust beneficiary to notify the bank of any assignment of the beneficial rights in the trust; otherwise the assignment is null and void. The trust agreement should include the following conditions for an assignment to be valid:

> The written consent of the bank.
> The fulfillment of all legal formalities required for the assignment.
> The payment of all taxes generated by the assignment.
> The property held in trust is current in all property taxes.

Example 3: Purchase of property outside of the restricted zone. The parties in example 3 above are actually executing a sales agreement. In these cases, the preferred contract is a **reserve title agreement** *(contrato con reserva de dominio)*, which is similar to a **land contract** in the United States. This type of contract is explained in detail in the section on reserve title and installment agreements.

REGISTRATION OF PROMISSORY AGREEMENTS

As a general rule, promissory agreements are not registered at the public registry: a promissory agreement does not affect real property rights over the property being sold. However, some public registries will register promissory agreements when possession of the property is delivered to the future buyer upon the execution of the promissory agreement.

When the promissory agreement cannot be registered it is common and legal to file a lawsuit, without notifying the defendant, to indirectly obtain the registration of the agreement. The end result is similar to *lis pendens* or *lis imaginaria,* which notifies third parties of the existence of the contract and protects the interests of the future buyer.

STEP THREE: TITLE SEARCH

An adequate title search must be done on the property before making the final payment, particularly in remote or underdeveloped areas of Mexico. Sometimes information filed with the public registry is overlooked, even though a certificate of no encumbrances must be issued before the notary will record the transaction.

There are title insurance companies in the United States that cover real estate transactions in Mexico. However, a buyer should still read the policies carefully.

A buyer should hire an Attorney to do the title search. The reason for this is that only an Attorney can give a legal opinion that a buyer can hold him responsible for. A real estate agent should not do the title search. They are usually representing the seller and unlikely to do a careful study of the chain of title, particularly if the agent cannot read Spanish, and if they give the buyer false of incorrect information there is not much recourse. They are not licensed to give legal opinions so I can be very difficult to hold them responsible when one relies on that opinion. This is especially true if the buyer could have hired an attorney and simply chose not to.

STEP FOUR: CERTIFICATE OF NO ENCUMBRANCES

For the public notary to record the purchase sales agreement, he needs to see a certificate of no encumbrances from the public registry and a certificate of no tax liability from the tax authority for the property.

This working article is hosted by Law Mexico Publishing and may not be commercially reproduced without the permission of the copyright holder. http://lawmexico.com/publications.htm Copyright 2009 Dennis John Peyton.

The seller should obtain these certificates at his own expense, although very often the buyer is charged for them. The buyer should ask for copies of these documents before seriously committing to the transaction. Normally, neither the real estate agent nor the seller will bother to get these documents unless the buyer is serious. They will often insist on an earnest money deposit to defray the costs of obtaining the documents.

CERTIFICATE OF NO ENCUMBRANCES

If the seller is unwilling to provide a current certificate of no encumbrances, it can be obtained at the public registry. This is public information, so there is no reason for the registry to deny issuing such a certificate to any interested party.

The certificate of no encumbrances should include the following information:

➢ The number of years back the title search on the property goes.
➢ The surface area of the property, its classification (urban or rural), and a legal description, including whether the property is held under co-ownership.
➢ The metes and bounds of the property.
➢ Property filing information, including the page, volume and section numbers.
➢ The name of the owner and the date of acquisition.
➢ The name of the person who requested the certificate.
➢ The city and state where the certificate was issued.
➢ The time and date the certificate was issued.
➢ The fee paid for the certificate.
➢ The name and signature of the registrar.
➢ The official seal of the public registry.

These certificates contain useful information regarding both the property and the owner. If any of the information from the certificate does not agree with the information provided by the seller, a buyer should take care. If the discrepancies are not eliminated, the buyer should request a refund and look for another piece of property.

CERTIFICATE OF NO TAX LIABILITY

The certificate of no tax liability is used as proof of property tax payment at the time of the transaction. It is intended to show that there are no pending tax payments which may not show up on the certificate of no encumbrances.

The certificate is issued by the head of the property tax department of the general treasury of the municipality where the property is located.

The certificate should contain the following information:

➢ The classification of the property (urban or rural).
➢ The property tax registration number *(clave catastral)*.
➢ The tax appraisal value.
➢ The name of the owner.
➢ The period up to which taxes are paid, and the receipt number and date of the last payment.
➢ The signature of the department head and seal of the municipal treasury.

This certificate is simple to obtain. The seller is usually happy to provide a copy. If there is an outstanding tax payment, it should be paid before continuing with the transaction.

This working article is hosted by Law Mexico Publishing and may not be commercially reproduced without the permission of the copyright holder. http://lawmexico.com/publications.htm Copyright 2009 Dennis John Peyton.

ADDITIONAL DOCUMENTS

Normally the seller of the property will provide the public notary with all the necessary documents need to complete a real estate transaction. This is because the notary will not proceed with the transaction if any document required by law is not provided to him. Since the property is recorded in the name of the seller, it makes sense that he or she should have all the necessary documents which were required when the property was acquired and recorded in the public registry. These documents make up the set that are usually kept together as the title documents.

Most states require the following documents to be presented when filing a real estate transaction at the public registry:

➢ Property survey authorized by the tax real estate registry (*Direccion de Catastro*). This document is normally valid for six months from the date issued.
➢ Property appraisal issued by the State Appraisals Commission, banking institutions, or an authorized appraisal expert. This document is also normally valid for six months from the date issued.
➢ Declaration of real estate acquisition taxes paid when the property was acquired.
➢ Declaration of provisional income tax payment for the transfer of title.
➢ Certificate of no tax liabilities.
➢ In regard to rural land (*predios rusticos*), besides all the above mentioned requirements, a written authorization issued by the Agrarian authority must also be presented. This is to verify that the property is not *ejido* property or in any way subject to the laws that deal with social property. This is done to make sure there are no reasons the property should not be sold as private property.

The buyer is not responsible for the above information and all of these documents should be required by the public notary when the transaction is being recorded and notarized. To avoid delays and possibly confusion it might not be a bad idea to make sure the seller has all of the above documents before closing.

STEP FIVE: PROPERTY APPRAISAL

This section was written by Lic. Jorge Diez de Bonilla, a Corredor Público in Tijuana, Baja California.

In accordance with the law on real estate it is mandatory to produce a topographic survey/plot plan of the land and an official appraisal. This appraisal is done to estimate the commercial value of the property including raw land, lots, houses, subdivisions, federal maritime- terrestrial zone, commercial and industrial units, etc. A *"Corredor Publico"* (an attorney at law licensed by the Federal Execute) may act as an appraiser for the estimation of the commercial value of all kinds of personal and real properties. The Federal Law of Public Brokerage states:

SECTION 6th. The public broker (*Corredor Publico*) is entitled to... II. Act as an expert appraiser to estimate, quantify and express the value of the properties, service, rights and obligations submitted to his/her option, appointed by a private party or by order of competent authority.

Furthermore, Section 4th of the Regulations for the Federal Fiscal Code appoints *Corredores Publicos* to concur with certain local authorities and Banks for the appraisal of properties for fiscal purposes. There are other federal and local laws establishing the appointment of *Corredores* in the appraisal field.

This working article is hosted by Law Mexico Publishing and may not be commercially reproduced without the permission of the copyright holder. http://lawmexico.com/publications.htm Copyright 2009 Dennis John Peyton.

However, Banks are also authorized to produce appraisals. They use architects, civil engineers, and others duly registered and licensed by the National Bank Commission. The appraisals made in such manner will have some value and enforcement as those made by *Corredores Publicos* in accordance with Sec. 46 XXII of the Law of Credit Institution.

The difference between using *Corredor Publico* or a Bank is that a *Corredor Publico* will often report the fair market value of the property in a prompt and simple manner. He can also certify, as a commercial notary public, appraisals made by other qualified persons. Banks require more time to elaborate the appraisal. Both are legally accepted by government agencies and notaries for the transfer of any property.

STEP SIX: CHOICE PURCHASE-SALES AGREEMENT

As mentioned earlier, the purchase-sales agreement is the contract by which title to the property being sold is actually transferred to the buyer or held in his benefit in the case of real estate trusts or *fideicomisos*. The type of transaction carried out almost always determines the choice of contract. Although all real estate transactions have some common elements, some require special considerations and therefore the agreements will vary.

All of the contracts have one thing in common: the seller wants to sell his property for a certain price and the buyer agrees to purchase the property at that price. The variables involve the amount of time the buyer has to pay the sales price and when the title to the property is actually conveyed to the buyer. This section examines the following types of contracts:

➤ General purchase sales contract.
➤ Reserve title and installment sales agreement.
➤ Irrevocable real estate trust agreement.
➤ Assignment of beneficial trust rights.

In order to determine which contract is best, the following questions need to be answered:

➤ **Where is the property located?** If the property is located in the restricted zone, a **real estate trust agreement** is required. The only exception to this rule is property to be used for non-residential purposes. In such cases, a foreign-owned Mexican corporation is used instead of a real estate trust. See Chapter Two for more information on the use of Mexican corporations for this purpose. If the property is located outside of the restricted zone then a normal **purchase sales contract** is used.
➤ **How will the purchase price be paid?** If the purchase price is going to be paid in installments over a long period of time, a **reserve title agreement** is used.
➤ **Is the property currently held in a real estate trust?** If the property is already held in trust then a contract for the assignment of rights is used. If the property is not currently held in trust a real estate trust agreement is used.

All of the contracts mentioned above include the basic elements of a purchase sales agreement. They all require the immediate or eventual payment of the purchase price and the subsequent transfer of title to the buyer. The following section summarizes the basic provisions applicable to all purchase sales agreements.

This working article is hosted by Law Mexico Publishing and may not be commercially reproduced without the permission of the copyright holder. http://lawmexico.com/publications.htm Copyright 2009 Dennis John Peyton.

General Provisions

When the Contract is Perfected

Generally speaking, purchase-sales agreements *(compraventa)* occur when one of the contracting parties obligates himself to transfer the ownership of property or trust rights, and the other agrees to pay a certain price for such property or rights. In theory, the contract is perfected and binding between the parties as soon as the property and its price are agreed upon, even when the property has not been delivered and the price has yet to be paid. For this reason, it is important that the seller and buyer recognize in writing, as soon as possible, that a formal contract must be drawn up to reflect the details of the sale, and that the parties still have not fully consented to the sale and purchase of the property being sold.

Requirements for an Agreement to Exists and be Valid

All purchase-sales agreements must meet specific requirements to legally exist and to be valid. Such requirements are known as essential elements and elements of validity.

The essential elements of any purchase-sales agreement are:

➢ **Consent:** acceptance or approval of what is planned or done by another. In a purchase-sales agreement, the seller grants consent by agreeing to transfer title to real property to the buyer. In turn, the buyer grants consent by agreeing to a certain price.

➢ **Object of the contract:** the purpose, aim, or goal of the contract. In a purchase-sales agreement, the purpose is to transfer title to real property to a buyer and to transfer a certain amount of money to the seller. The indirect object of the contract is the property and the price.

The contract is declared null, having no legal force, if it does not include the price, or if the property does not exist. To legally exist, the property must physically exist and it must be included in objects of commerce. In other words, the property can be seen and identified. To be "included in commerce" means that the property may be sold—it is not federally owned property or affected in any other law or defect that would hinder or prohibit its sale.

There are properties that either by law or by their nature cannot be acquired. Such properties are considered excluded from commerce. An object is considered excluded from commerce by its nature when an individual cannot possess it exclusively. It is considered excluded from commerce by provision of law when the law declares that the property cannot be reduced to private ownership.

The price can be stipulated as a payment in money or in some other personal or real property as long as such other property has legal value. The price must be fair. The law states that **when someone acquires excessive profit by taking advantage of the ignorance, inexperience, or distressed state of another person, the disadvantaged person has the right to demand that the contract in question be declared null and void; or that there be an equitable reduction of their obligation, plus the payment of damages.**

The elements of validity of a purchase-sales agreement are as follows:

➢ **Legal capacity:** the legal rights the parties have to enter into the contract. Generally, one must be in control of his mental faculties and be an adult. In some real estate transactions, such as those involving properties in the restricted zone, the law also requires that the parties both be Mexican. Foreigners do not have the capacity to enter into a purchase-sales agreement in this instance due to provisions in Article 27 of the Constitution. For this reason a real estate trust is used.

This working article is hosted by Law Mexico Publishing and may not be commercially reproduced without the permission of the copyright holder. http://lawmexico.com/publications.htm Copyright 2009 Dennis John Peyton.

> **Legal Form:** All purchase-sales agreements for real estate transactions must be in writing. In order for the transaction to be binding before third parties, the agreement must also be recorded with a public notary and filed with the public registry.

In addition to the limits of legal capacity of foreigners in real estate transactions in the restricted zone, the following should also be considered:

> **Legal Capacity in the sale of co-owned property**: In sales of co-owned property, the other co-owners of the property have the right of first refusal when one of the other co-owners wants to sell his undivided share of the property. The law requires that the co-owner notify the other co-owners of sales through a notary or the courts, in order to allow them to exercise their right of first refusal. The legal term for exercising this right is eight days from date of notification or the co-owners lose this right. Any sale made without such notification is null and void and has no legal effect whatsoever. If several co-owners are interested in exercising their right of first refusal, the co-owner with the greater share in the property is given preference. If they have equal shares, the co-owner is designated by lot, unless agreed otherwise.
> **Capacity of husband or wife:** A marriage partner must have the consent of the other spouse to enter into a contract to sell real estate if the marriage is designated as under community property *(sociedad conyugal).*
> **Capacity of Parents of children:** Parents of children who are under their parental power must get consent from the courts to sell property owned by the children.

PAYMENT AND INTEREST FOR LATE PAYMENT

The buyer must pay the sales price according to the terms and within the time stipulated in his agreement with the seller. If the agreement makes no specific indication, it is assumed that the payment will be made in cash. If the buyer delays payment he may be required to pay **interest at the legal rate** (9% annually) on the amount due. In all cases involving interest payments, the parties may use a higher percentage as long as it is not excessive.

LUMP SUM SALES

Generally, if one or more pieces of real property is sold for a lump sum *(precio alzado)*, without determining its parts or measuring the properties involved, neither of the parties to the agreement may rescind the contract based on a deficit or excess upon the delivery of the property. A lump sum payment refers to a transaction in which a single sum of money serves as complete payment for several distinct parcels of real estate. These are also known as *ad corpus* sales. The basic idea is that the buyer and the seller agree to the sale of the property or properties "as is" without being held to a specific calculation or measurement.

PAYMENT OF TRANSACTION OR CLOSING COSTS

The law states that the parties shall each pay one-half of the costs of the instruments of sale and registry unless otherwise agreed. These costs are normally notary fees and public registry filing fees. The law does not specifically mention other costs; therefore, each party is responsible for his transaction costs, such as legal fees and the like. However, by mutual consent, these costs and any other fees and expenses may be designated the responsibility of one of the parties. For example, in a "seller's market" the buyer may agree to pay all transaction costs.

MULTIPLE SALES ON A SINGLE PROPERTY

If the same seller sells a property to several buyers, the following provisions are observed:

This working article is hosted by Law Mexico Publishing and may not be commercially reproduced without the permission of the copyright holder. http://lawmexico.com/publications.htm Copyright 2009 Dennis John Peyton.

> If the sale involves **personal property**, *(bienes muebles)* the first sale will prevail over those that were carried out later. If the time of the transaction cannot be determined, the sale executed by the person who is in possession of the property shall prevail.
> If the sale involves **real property**, the sale first registered with the public registry will prevail. If none has been registered, the above rules covering personal property apply.

Priority and Good Faith Acquisitions

There is a fundamental rule: a **person can only sell property that he owns.** The sale of property that is owned by another person is void unless the person selling the property is representing the owner. If the sale resulted from fraud or bad faith, the seller is liable for damages and losses caused by the sale.

On the other hand, if the buyer acquired the property in good faith, the provisions relating to the public registry must be taken into account. These provisions state that a record of a transaction in the public registry protects the rights acquired in good faith by a third party, even if the right of the party executing them is later annulled or rescinded.

The only exceptions to this rule are:

> When the cause of the nullity appears clearly in the same registry.
> When the contract used required no payment to change hands in the transaction.
> When the executed contracts are in violation of the law.

However, if the seller acquires ownership of the property by any legal title before dispossession takes place, the contract is validated.

Sale of Property Under Litigation

Property under litigation may be sold. However, the law requires that the seller of such property tell the buyer of the existence of the litigation. If the seller does not inform the buyer, the seller is liable for damages and losses if the buyer suffers dispossession. If the buyer is informed of the litigation on the property at the time of purchase, and is subsequently deprived of title due to the outcome of the litigation, the seller is not responsible for damages and losses the buyer incurs.

Personal Restrictions on Certain Buyers

The law prohibits certain people from buying property due to their personal legal relationship to the seller. The following fall into this category:

> Magistrates, judges, the district attorney, official defenders, lawyers, prosecutors and experts cannot buy the property affected by litigation in which they take part, nor can they be assignees of rights relating to such property. The exceptions to this rule are hereditary property in which they are co-heirs or properties where the property rights belong to them.
> Children subject to parental rights *(patria potestad)* can only sell to their parents property which, according to the law, they have acquired by their own labors.
> Owners of an undivided property cannot sell their respective share without notifying the other co-owners so that they may exercise the right of first refusal to buy the property.
> Experts *(peritos)* and brokers *(corredores)* cannot buy property in the sale of which they have intervened.
> The following persons may not purchase the property which they have been entrusted to sell or administrate: guardians and curators; agents; testamentary executors and those appointed in case of intestacy; inspectors appointed by the testator or by the heirs; representatives, administrators and inspectors in case of absence; public employees.

This working article is hosted by Law Mexico Publishing and may not be commercially reproduced without the permission of the copyright holder. http://lawmexico.com/publications.htm Copyright 2009 Dennis John Peyton.

Any sales made in violation of the above provisions, whether made directly or through another person, are void.

OBLIGATIONS OF THE SELLER

The law provides for three basic obligations of the seller:

➤ To deliver the property sold to the buyer;
➤ To guarantee the quality of the property;
➤ To guarantee his title.

The extent of these obligations is determined by the purchase-sales contract. The last obligation refers to the seller's obligation to compensate the buyer in the event the buyer is disturbed in his right to quiet enjoyment of purchased property through foreclosure or similar proceedings.

DELIVERY OF THE PROPERTY

The Civil Code identifies delivery as **real, juridical or virtual delivery.** Real or actual delivery consists of conveying material possession of the property to the buyer, or of assigning the title documents, in cases concerning the sale of trust rights, to the buyer.

Juridical, or "constructive delivery" as it is known in the United States, occurs when, without actual delivery, the law considers the property as having been received by the buyer. This means that the seller has made the property available to the buyer for his use and enjoyment. From the moment that the buyer accepts the property at his disposition, he is regarded as having virtually received it, and if the seller retains it in his possession he has only the rights and obligations of a depository.

The seller is not obligated to deliver the property if the buyer has not paid for it, unless a designated time of payment is provided in the contract. The seller is not obligated to deliver property if, during such time, the buyer becomes insolvent, thus endangering the payment unless the buyer posts a bond to guarantee payment when due. Proof of insolvency must be such that there is imminent danger that the seller will not receive payment.

As a general rule, the property is delivered in the condition it was in at the time the contract was completed. This rule is warranted because the buyer is considered the owner of the property from the moment the contract is completed. For this reason, the two events—contract completion and property delivery—often coincide. In cases where improvements have yet to be completed, the contract should state that such improvements must be made before delivery is taken.

OBLIGATIONS OF THE BUYER

The principle obligation of the buyer is to comply with the terms of the purchase-sales contract, most importantly, the obligation to pay the seller in the place, time and form agreed upon. If no place and time are set in the contract, the law requires that payment be made at the time and place of delivery. In case of doubt as to which party should deliver first, the property and money should both be deposited with a third party.

The law requires the buyer to pay interest between the time of delivery and the time of payment in the following cases:

➤ When the parties so agree.
➤ When the buyer receives benefit from the property in the form of produce or income before he has fulfilled his obligation of payment as stipulated in the purchase-sales contract. The

This working article is hosted by Law Mexico Publishing and may not be commercially reproduced without the permission of the copyright holder. http://lawmexico.com/publications.htm Copyright 2009 Dennis John Peyton.

law compensates the seller because the buyer has received benefit from the property without paying for it. In cases of installment sales without stipulation for interest, the buyer is not liable for interest, even if he has received the benefit from the property. The law assumes that the parties took the term of the contract into consideration when setting the price.

➤ When a term for payment is granted after the execution of the purchase-sales contract, the buyer must pay interest from the date the contract was executed unless otherwise agreed.

➤ When the buyer is in default in fixed term payments.

GENERAL PURCHASE-SALES AGREEMENT

A purchase-sales agreement is the contract by which title to real estate is conveyed. If the value of the real estate sale does not exceed the equivalent of three hundred and sixty-five times the minimum salary in effect in the Federal District at the moment of the operation, the parties may execute the sale in a private agreement. In this case, two people must witness the signatures of the seller and the buyer, and then their signatures are ratified before a notary public, a Justice of the Peace, or the Public Registry. Most real estate transactions exceed this limit. The rule is only intended as a general method of procedure because the actual amount is set by the Civil Code of the state where the property is located.

Regardless of the provisions of the state Civil Code, the use of a private agreement is not recommended. The transaction should always be done before a notary. The buyer will need to eventually record and file the transaction anyway, if the transaction is to be binding before third parties. Therefore, it is never worth taking a chance by not recording the transaction no matter what the seller or the real estate agent may say.

If the parties celebrating the contract cannot write, another person with legal capacity may sign in their name at their request, with the exception of the witnesses of the transaction. The fingerprint *(huella digital)* of the party who did not sign is then impressed on the document.

Typically, the notary public who records the purchase-sale agreement also draws up the agreement. If there are any particular provisions that need to be included, an English translation of the agreement should be done. In any event, if the buyer does not speak Spanish it is almost always worth having an English translation done of the agreement. Such translations should be done by a *perito traductor*, or the translation should be reviewed or done by a Mexican attorney.

RESERVE TITLE AND INSTALLMENT SALES CONTRACTS

In a reserve title agreement the seller reserves title or ownership to the property until payment is made in full, however, the buyer is allowed to take possession, and may use and enjoy the property while payments are being made. More often than not reserve title agreements will include installment payments. The advantages of using this type of contract are twofold:

➤ It can be registered at the Public Registry, therefore it is binding before third parties.

➤ The seller may not sell the property as long as the buyer is in compliance with the agreement. This usually means that the buyer is current in his payments to the seller.

In a reserve title agreement the obligations of the parties are subject to a **suspensive condition**, which, in other words, is a condition which prevents a contract from going into operation until it has been fulfilled. This type of condition is the opposite of a **resolutory condition** which is that which, when accomplished, operates the revocation of the obligation, placing matters in the same state as though the obligation had not existed.

This working article is hosted by Law Mexico Publishing and may not be commercially reproduced without the permission of the copyright holder. http://lawmexico.com/publications.htm Copyright 2009 Dennis John Peyton.

In a reserve title agreement this means that the obligations to convey title take effect from the day on which they were contracted, but they cannot be enforced until a certain event takes place. In a reserve title contract, this event is usually the final payment to the seller from the buyer.

During the period of the installment payments, the buyer is considered the conditional owner of the property. As long as the buyer complies with the conditions of the agreement, title is transferred on the date full payment is made, as in any other real estate sale. However, if payment is not made, then the buyer is considered a lessee for the time he held the property.

When the property is sold under a reserve title agreement, the agreement is enforceable against third persons only if it is registered in the Public Registry.

Sales agreements in which the buyer makes **installment payments (*abonos*)** are subject to the following rules:

➢ In sales of real property it may be stipulated that the seller may rescind the contract if the buyer fails to pay one or more installments. However, in order for the rescission to be effective against third parties who have acquired the property from the buyer in spite of the installment sales contract, the contract must be registered in the public registry.
➢ In the sale of personal property which can be positively identified, the same clause for rescission may be stipulated, and it is also only effective against third parties acquiring the property when the contract has been registered in the public registry.
➢ In case of personal property which cannot be positively identified, and therefore cannot be registered, the parties may stipulate that the contract may be rescinded upon failure to pay the sales price, but this clause is not enforceable against third persons acquiring the property in good faith.

If the sale is rescinded, the buyer and seller must make reciprocal restitution of whatever has been received. However, when the seller has delivered the property sold to the buyer, the seller may require the buyer to pay rent for the period of time the buyer had possession of the property. The amount of rent is predetermined either by the parties in the contract or by experts, if the contract does not include such provisions or if the rent stipulated in the contract is excessive. The seller is also entitled to payment for any damages the property has suffered. If the buyer has paid part of the price, he may be entitled to legal interest (9% annually) on the amount paid. Any agreements imposing obligations on the buyer more onerous than those expressed shall be void.

In installment contracts, the buyer may withhold payment if he is disturbed or justly fears disturbance in his possession, until the seller guarantees the buyer's possession. On the other hand, unjustified failure to make payment entitles the seller to sue for the rescission of the installment contract.

IRREVOCABLE REAL ESTATE TRUST AGREEMENT

The irrevocable real estate trust agreement, or *el fideicomiso*, is the most common way to take title to property in the restricted zone. For a review of what constitutes the restricted zone and parties involved in a real estate trust agreement see Chapter Two, and Condominiums in the restricted zone in Chapter Fourteen.

TRUST PERMIT PROCESS

A Mexican bank must obtain a trust permit from the Ministry of Foreign Affairs to set up an irrevocable real estate trust. The buyer and the seller must provide the bank/trustee with the following information:

This working article is hosted by Law Mexico Publishing and may not be commercially reproduced without the permission of the copyright holder. http://lawmexico.com/publications.htm Copyright 2009 Dennis John Peyton.

- ➢ Name, address and nationality of trustor(s) (This is the person who is selling the property).
- ➢ Name, address and nationality of beneficiary(ies).
- ➢ Title documents for the property to be held in trust. Most often producing a recorded and registered deed to the property *(escrituras)* accomplishes this. These documents also include a legal description of the property as well as its location, surface area, and metes and bounds. The bank/trustee may not require that the seller or the buyer produce the deed to the property but rather only a legal description of the property, its location, surface area, and metes and bounds; however, a buyer at this point in the transaction should already have a copy of the *deed*. If not, he should get one immediately. The trust permit process should not proceed until a current copy of the *deed* is obtained and the buyer is satisfied that there are no problems with the title to the property.
- ➢ A survey of the property *(croquis)*.
- ➢ The distance the property is located from the federal zone. If the property adjoins the federal zone, trust permits now require the beneficiary to allow access to the federal zone via any established public access.
- ➢ A letter of intent indicating the amount that will be invested in improving the property when the total surface area is more than 2000 square meters.

With the above information the bank/trustee can apply for a trust permit. The application also includes the following conditions:

- ➢ The intended use of the property. In this case, the intended use is residential. If the property is not to be used for residential purposes, a buyer should consider using a Mexican corporation to hold the property instead of a real estate trust. See Chapter Two for more information.
- ➢ The beneficiary agrees to the inclusion of the *clausula calvo*. This means that they will consider themselves as Mexican with regard to the rights they have in the property and not invoke the intervention of their government with regard to those rights.
- ➢ If the beneficiary assigns the trust rights contained in the real estate trust, the bank/trustee must obtain authorization from the Ministry of Foreign Affairs for the new beneficiaries of the trust.
- ➢ The beneficiaries must notify the bank/trustee of compliance with the purpose of the trust and any other conditions agreed to in the trust agreement. The bank/trustee informs the Ministry of Foreign Affairs of such compliance.
- ➢ The bank/trustee must notify the Ministry of Foreign Affairs of any cancellation of a trust within 90 working days.
- ➢ The beneficiaries and the bank/trustee agree that any violation of the conditions contained in the trust permit may result in the cancellation and liquidation of the trust within 180 days of notification.
- ➢ If the trust beneficiary instructs the bank/trustee to lease the property held in trust to foreigners or Mexican corporations with foreign participation, prior authorization must be obtained from the Ministry of Foreign Affairs.
- ➢ The duration of the trust is that established by the Foreign Investment Law (50 years) and it can be renewed before the term of the contract lapses.
- ➢ The Ministry of Foreign Affairs reserves the right to verify compliance with the conditions agreed to in the trust permit.
- ➢ The use of the trust permit implies the unconditional acceptance of its terms and conditions.

All banks/trustees require a trust permit fee depending on the duration of the trust. This fee is paid to the government and is periodically adjusted. The fees are paid in new pesos. I have

This working article is hosted by Law Mexico Publishing and may not be commercially reproduced without the permission of the copyright holder. http://lawmexico.com/publications.htm Copyright 2009 Dennis John Peyton.

converted the amount to dollars because the dollar amounts usually stay about the same over time. The approximate permit fee to the government $1,000 US for a fifty year permit

Another governmental fee that is required is the foreign investment registration. This is a one time fee which is about $150 US, but can vary because banks have had trouble avoiding late fees which can increase this to $800 US.

DRAFTING AND EXECUTION OF THE TRUST AGREEMENT

Once the bank/trustee obtains the trust permit from the Ministry of Foreign Affairs, an irrevocable real estate trust agreement is drawn up, usually by the bank/trustee or the public notary who works with the bank/trustee. The parties are then notified to execute the agreement before the public notary.

The following will be required for the notary to begin the recording process:

1. Title documents for the property to be held in trust.

2. A certificate of no tax liability.

3. A certificate of no encumbrances.

4. Topographic studies of the property.

5. An appraisal of the property.

The seller provides items 1 through 4. A bank appraiser or a public broker completes item 5.

The contractual relations for executing the trust agreement are between the seller of the property as trustor and the bank as trustee. The beneficiary of the trust is represented by the bank/trustee and does not execute the trust agreement. However, the principle rights and obligations of the beneficiary—the person buying the property, are contained in the trust agreement. For this reason it is important that the buyer understand what is contained in the agreement before the bank/trustee and the seller sign it. The buyer is the one who will have to live with the terms and conditions of the trust agreement.

Once the seller signs the trust agreement, title to the property is conveyed to the bank as trustee. Since there is not much in the law concerning trust agreements, most of the buyer's rights and obligations are laid out in the trust agreement. As in any contractual relationship, it is always better to make any changes or adjustments before the contract is executed.

Since a trust agreement is a contract, many of its terms and conditions can be modified. Unfortunately, many do not take the time to find out what the agreement contains. Most of the banks do not offer an English translation of the trust agreement, and the typical buyer believes it is beyond his comprehension and so chooses not to delve into the mysteries of the contract.

A buyer should always get a translation of the contract done or he should have a Mexican attorney review it. Most Mexican contracts, including a trust agreement, are pretty straightforward and easy to understand. A buyer who takes the time to review the contract, is not only able to get the most favorable bank fees but also has a better understanding of what he can and cannot do with the property held in trust.

Most trust agreements are essentially the same, although there may be some slight changes from one bank/trustee to another. The following is intended to apprise a buyer of the most common elements of the trust agreement and the alternatives available.

The bank that is acting as trustee should be able to provide a copy of the trust permit and a sample trust agreement for review. Some banks are starting to make sample English versions

This working article is hosted by Law Mexico Publishing and may not be commercially reproduced without the permission of the copyright holder. http://lawmexico.com/publications.htm Copyright 2009 Dennis John Peyton.

available but more often there is only a Spanish copy. A Mexican attorney working with a buyer may be able to have an English translation done for a minimal fee, or even include the translation in the legal fee for setting up the trust.

It is important to obtain copies of both the trust permit and the trust agreement itself, since these two documents include almost all of the buyer's rights and obligations. The final recorded version of the trust agreement will probably not look the same as the copies obtained from the bank/trustee but it will contain the same information. The text of the trust permit is copied to the final recorded trust agreement, and the actual clauses of the agreement are the same as what the bank/trustee provided.

SPECIAL CONSIDERATIONS FOR THE TRUST AGREEMENT

The information contained in the trust permit cannot be changed. It should be similar to the outline above. The trust agreement itself, as with any contract, may be modified. The part of the agreement that reads *"CLAUSULAS"* is where the clauses of the contract start. If there are other sections before this section, this is not a cause for concern; those sections are for filing purposes and declarations regarding background information on the property.

OBJECT, CONSIDERATION AND WARRANTIES

Usually, the first few clauses deal with the purpose of the trust, the consideration, or the amount paid for the property, and warranties against hidden defects. These clauses should state that the trust is irrevocable and that the real estate held in trust is conveyed without any reservation or limitation.

The trustor/seller is also responsible by law for any hidden defects of title relative to the real estate in trust, and binds himself to pay any indebtedness affecting the real estate in trust previous to the date of the trust agreement.

The consideration *(contraprestación)* should be the full amount paid for the property. There have been many transactions recorded with a sales price lower than what was actually paid, supposedly to save on tax payments. This is tax evasion and should not be accepted for any reason. In such cases, the buyer is considered a party to defrauding the Mexican tax authorities.

It is foolish to run such a risk considering that the benefit to the buyer is very small since the buyer only pays a 2% acquisition tax. The buyer usually ends up paying these taxes anyway when he sells the property due to the low base price used when determining the capital gain created by the sale of the property. If it appears that the property was bought for 5, when it was actually 10, when it is sold for 15 the taxable gain is 10. That translates into 50% more taxes. It is not in the interest of the buyer to use a lower sales price. A buyer only stands to lose in this situation.

DESIGNATION OF BENEFICIARY AND SUBSTITUTE BENEFICIARY

Usually the above clauses are followed by a clause to designate the trust's beneficiaries and substitute beneficiaries. Some banks will include this information in one of the first few clauses instead of including it in a clause of its own.

It is important to clearly understand the differences between the two beneficiaries and how they are used in the trust agreement.

The beneficiary of the trust is the person who has the right to use and enjoy the property held in trust and to give instructions to the bank/trustee with regard to the property. There may be one or more beneficiaries. When there is more than one, all of them are treated as co-owners and the

This working article is hosted by Law Mexico Publishing and may not be commercially reproduced without the permission of the copyright holder. http://lawmexico.com/publications.htm Copyright 2009 Dennis John Peyton.

legal provisions regarding co-ownership regulate their rights and obligations to the property. For more information on co-ownership see Chapter Thirteen.

Substitute beneficiaries, on the other hand, are not co-owners, at least not immediately. A substitute beneficiary is only intended to take the place of the actual beneficiary upon the beneficiary's death. A substitute beneficiary does not have any rights to the property held in trust until he becomes an actual trust beneficiary due to the death of the beneficiary.

The reason for having substitute beneficiaries is to avoid having to go through probate to have the trust rights assigned to the decedent's heirs. By including a substitute beneficiary, there is no question as to who is the heir to the trust rights.

When there is more than one beneficiary it is essential that the trust agreement clearly indicate that each substitute beneficiary takes the place of the beneficiary for which he was designated upon the death of such beneficiary. Moreover, the agreement should also indicate that the other beneficiaries agree to such substitution and renounce any rights they may have as co-owners of the trust rights. This is to avoid any confusion as to who has the right to the decedent's rights in the trust upon his death.

Many of the trust agreements do not include this distinction and therefore leave open the possibility that one of the other co-owners has the right to the decedent's interests in the trust instead of the substitute beneficiary. This is especially a problem when a spouse is a co-beneficiary in the trust and their children are named as substitute beneficiaries.

Although there are many methods to determine who has the right to the decedent's interest in the trust, the best one is to make the intentions clear from the beginning. If there is any doubt, the final answer is determined by a judge; which then makes the whole point of designating a substitute beneficiary meaningless.

PURPOSES OF THE TRUST

Every trust agreement includes a clause that lists the purposes of the trust. The following list is a typical example of what is included in this type of clause:

➢ The stipulation that the bank/trustee holds title to the property of the real estate in trust.
➢ The specification that the beneficiaries have the rights to use and exercise their rights in the property as it best suits their interests, always subject to the provisions of all applicable laws.
➢ The provision that the bank/trustee can lease the real estate in trust for periods not longer than 10 years. In this case, the beneficiary shall receive the income that such lease creates.
➢ The specification that the bank/trustee transfers the ownership of the real estate held in trust to the beneficiaries themselves or to any individual or corporation that has the power to acquire the real estate according to the law. In all cases, the proceeds from the real estate should transfer to the beneficiaries or their assigns.
➢ The stipulation that, upon beneficiary's request, the bank/trustee shall grant a mortgage security in the real estate in trust to secure the obligations contracted by the beneficiary; in the title granting the security, it should be noted that the bank/trustee does not contract any payment obligation.
➢ The provision that, upon termination of the trust, the bank/trustee transfers the real estate ownership to the individual or legal entity legally empowered to acquire it, delivering to the beneficiaries the proceeds of the real estate transfers.

It should be noted that leasing and mortgaging the property held in trust is possible. The limit of ten years for leases is set by law and is applicable to residential properties.

This working article is hosted by Law Mexico Publishing and may not be commercially reproduced without the permission of the copyright holder. http://lawmexico.com/publications.htm Copyright 2009 Dennis John Peyton.

RIGHT TO MAKE IMPROVEMENTS

The trust agreement should also contain a clause that allows the beneficiary to make improvements on the property. This includes any kind of construction permitted by law.

The agreement normally includes provisions that limit the liabilities related to the improvements to the beneficiary. To do this, provisions similar to the following are included as obligations of the beneficiary:

➢ Negotiate on behalf of the bank/trustee the licenses, permits, appraisals, etc., required, provided that the beneficiary shall assume all liability for possible violations of legislation concerning construction, as well as any other responsibility derived from work, construction or improvements to the existing property.

➢ Give termination notice and any other pertinent information, also on behalf of the bank/trustee.

➢ Notify the bank/trustee periodically regarding improvements made so that the bank/trustee may increase the value of the property held in trust and make the necessary accounting entries.

RIGHTS OF THE BENEFICIARY

The specific rights of the beneficiary are usually contained in a clause and identified as such. However, sometimes these rights are sprinkled throughout the agreement. Either way, as long as they are included in the agreement the effect is the same. The following are the most essential rights and should be included in every trust agreement:

➢ **Right to modify or amend the trust agreement** in whole or in part at any time. Any change to the trust agreement must be with the prior written consent of the bank/trustee and be recorded before a public notary. Such changes must not infringe upon provisions of the Foreign Investment Law or any other applicable law.

➢ **Right to assign or encumber the beneficial trust rights** in any manner. In order that the bank/trustee recognize any assignment or encumbrance of the trust rights, the following shall be required:

1. A notarial notification to the bank/trustee.

2. In the event the beneficiary assigns his rights, such assignment shall be made by a notary public and the bank/trustee shall appear before him in order to accept the assignment.

3. Fulfillment of the provisions set forth in the trust agreement.

➢ **Right to mortgage on the real estate in trust**. Upon the beneficiary's request, the bank/trustee must proceed to grant a mortgage on the real estate in trust in order to secure the obligations contracted by said beneficiary. Within the instrument establishing the security interest, it should be noted that the bank/trustee is not obligated in any manner and simply agrees, upon the beneficiary's request, to encumber the property held in trust.

TAXES AND OTHER OBLIGATIONS

Taxes or any other obligations derived from the real estate held in trust are the responsibility of the beneficiary. As such, the trust agreement will include provisions that require the beneficiary to prove to the bank/trustee's satisfaction that he has fulfilled all outstanding obligations before assignment or termination of the trust agreement.

The bank/trustee is not obliged to defend the ownership of the property in trust. However, the trust agreement should state that upon receipt of any notice, judicial complaint, or any demand concerning the real estate in trust, the bank/trustee must promptly notify the beneficiary or the

This working article is hosted by Law Mexico Publishing and may not be commercially reproduced without the permission of the copyright holder. http://lawmexico.com/publications.htm Copyright 2009 Dennis John Peyton.

attorney designated for that purpose. This is so the defense of the ownership may be assumed by the beneficiary through his lawyers. It is best if this notification is made in writing and allows enough time for the beneficiary to act accordingly.

If the beneficiary is difficult to reach, it is advisable that a Mexican attorney be appointed to receive such notifications. The attorney should be granted a power of attorney for lawsuits and recovery so that he is able to take immediate action if necessary. It is also prudent to include provisions in the trust agreement that indicate that the bank/trustee shall grant powers for administrative acts and/or for process and collections in favor of the person named by the beneficiary.

The beneficiary or his attorney should attend to such notifications quickly because normally the notification terminates any liability of the bank/trustee to act on behalf of the beneficiary. In case of litigation time may be very important and deadlines can be missed if action is not taken immediately.

DURATION OF THE TRUST

The law gives the following causes for the termination of a trust:

The trust is extinguished:

1. By the fulfillment of the purpose for which it was constituted.

2. By such fulfillment being impossible.

3. By the impossibility of fulfilling the suspensive condition on which the trust depends, or for not having used the trust within the term specified for its establishment or, in its default, within a term of twenty years following its establishment. Strictly speaking, in this case the trust is not extinguished but rather it never comes into existence.

4. By having fulfilled the resolutory condition to which the trust had been subject to.

5. By an express agreement between the trustor and the beneficiary of the trust. This would not be applicable in most real estate trusts in the restricted zone because those trusts are irrevocable.

6. By revocation made by trustor, when he has expressly reserved such right at the time the trust was created.

7. When the trust is constituted in favor of the fiduciary.

The trust may be for a term of up to 50 years and may expire for any of the reasons listed above as long as they are consistent with the provisions of the trust agreement. Therefore it is important that the trust agreement clearly indicate that the trustor/seller does not reserve the right to revoke the trust as provided for in # 6 above. In other words, all real estate trusts in the restricted zone should always be irrevocable and this should be clear indicated in the agreement.

The agreement should state that upon termination of the established term, the bank/trustee shall proceed, as instructed by the beneficiary, to sell the real estate to the individual or corporation having legal capacity to acquire the property. The beneficiary or his assigns shall receive the proceeds of such sale. If the beneficiary does not instruct the bank/trustee concerning the disposition of the property in trust, when the established term expires, the bank/trustee shall order a real estate appraisal with an authorized credit institution. The bank/trustee shall then proceed to sell the real estate through a public broker, delivering its proceeds to the beneficiary or its assign.

This working article is hosted by Law Mexico Publishing and may not be commercially reproduced without the permission of the copyright holder. http://lawmexico.com/publications.htm Copyright 2009 Dennis John Peyton.

A beneficiary should read the trust agreement carefully. Very often the bank/trustee will include a 5% commission on the sale of the property upon the termination of the trust's term if the beneficiary has not given any other instructions.

BANK/TRUSTEE FEES

One of the most important sections in the trust agreement is that which deals with the various fees the bank/trustee charges for maintaining the trust. The fees charged by banks can differ greatly--a buyer should take the time to find out what the bank/trustee is charging and compare it to other banks.

The following is a guideline for determining the different concepts and approximate values to be applied to each:

➢ Review and acceptance of trust payable upon the signing of the trust agreement: $350 to $750 US

➢ Annual administration: 0.20 to 1% of the value of the property held in trust per annum, or a minimum of $350 to $3,300 US payable annually. One should expect to pay 1% for properties valued at $25,000 US and below. The rate of .20% is reserved for properties valued at $1,000,000 and above. The fee is reduced at a rate of 0.05% for each $35,000 increase in the value of the property until 0.45% and $350,000 is reached. From this point to one million dollars the rate is reduced 0.05% for each $170,000 increase in the value of the property.

➢ Execution of private titles and contracts different from the trust agreement and of acts not provided for in the trust agreement, $250 to $500 US for each execution.

➢ Up to 3% moratory interest per month, if trust fees are not paid on time and while these remain unpaid.

➢ Up to 1% of the recorded value of the property or of the sales price, which ever is higher, for the assignment of trust rights. Sometimes this fee is waived; it doesn't hurt to ask!

Most of the banks are beginning to adjust the property values of trusts on a yearly basis. However, the bank/trustee may make these adjustments sooner, especially if the property is being sold. At any rate, the bank trust fees normally are due and payable once a year.

The bank/trustee will normally include provisions in the trust agreement, which guarantee the payment of their fees. The provision usually specifies that the bank discontinue performance of any administrative procedure, or any partial or whole cancellation of this trust, while there is any fee indebtedness or any other fee in favor of the bank/trustee. All fees, together with the corresponding value added taxes, must be paid by the beneficiary before any such actions can take place.

REPORTING REQUIREMENTS TO BANK/TRUSTEE

The amounts charged by the bank are calculated using the bank appraised value of the property, therefore, a beneficiary must know what reporting obligations he has with regard to improvements. Most trust agreements require that the beneficiary notify the bank/trustee of improvements made to the property within 15 days. Some banks will also require notification if any bank appraisal is done on the property, also within the 15-day limit.

ASSIGNMENT OF RIGHTS AGREEMENT

This type of agreement (*cesion de derechos*) is used when the property being purchased is already held in trust. It is an assignment of rights because the buyer is actually purchasing the beneficial rights the seller has in the real estate trust which holds title to the property.

This working article is hosted by Law Mexico Publishing and may not be commercially reproduced without the permission of the copyright holder. http://lawmexico.com/publications.htm Copyright 2009 Dennis John Peyton.

In order for the assignment to be legal it must be carried out before a public notary or a public broker and it must abide by the terms and conditions of the trust agreement. The bank/trustee also needs to notify the Ministry of Foreign Affairs so that the assignment may be authorized and the new beneficiary can agree to the calvo clause.

First, when purchasing a property that is held in trust, the buyer should ask the seller for a copy of the seller's trust agreement. Since the buyer is purchasing the rights contained in this agreement he should review it to see if it meets the standards laid out above in the previous sections on trust agreements. If there are changes to be made this is the time to request them.

The bank/trustee fees should be reasonable. In some cases, the fees were set years ago and are very reasonable. Trusts established in the late 1980's, on the other hand, sometimes set fees much higher because of the government bank monopoly, which existed throughout that decade. A buyer will want to check around to get an idea of what the current fees are then ask to have his adjusted accordingly.

Both the beneficiary and the substitute beneficiary need to be changed. As mentioned earlier, the substitute beneficiary is important and should not be left out. If the substitute beneficiary is left blank there will be an additional fee to add one later.

The parties to the assignment of rights contract are either the seller/beneficiary and the buyer or the bank/trustee and the buyer. Under no circumstances should the buyer accept an assignment of trust rights without the consent of the bank/trustee.

Over the years there have been many assignment contracts executed without the knowledge or consent of the bank/trustee, even some that have been recorded and filed with the Public Registry. But, it should always be remembered that it is the buyer who has to deal with the bank in the future. Once the seller is paid he may disappear. Therefore it is in the buyer's interests to make sure that the bank/trustee is fully aware of and consents to the assignment of trust rights.

There are many arguments regarding the need to inform the bank concerning the assignment of trust rights. Some believe it is not necessary since the assignment concerns personal property rights, rather than real property rights, therefore, the transaction may be executed in a private agreement. These arguments must not persuade a prospective buyer. The main concern is to comply with the conditions set forth in the trust permit and the trust agreement. More importantly, a buyer does not want to fight with the bank/trustee to have his rights recognized nor does he want to discover after the transaction that the seller still owes bank trust fees!

To avoid all of these situations, the buyer must ensure the assignment of rights agreement includes the consent of the bank/trustee and authorization from the Ministry of Foreign Affairs. By doing so he can rest assured that he will be registered as the new beneficiary of the trust and that all trust fees are current.

If the seller has chosen to the have the bank/trustee represent him in the assignment, the bank's trust representative will execute the contract with the buyer before a public notary or a public broker. If the seller is executing the assignment agreement, consent from the bank/trustee is granted through a letter of instruction sent to the notary or the public broker.

The contents of the assignment should be similar to the trust agreement. After all, all of the rights the buyer is purchasing are contained in that agreement--the assignment only recognizes the transfer.

If the trust agreement needs to be changed this would be the time to address such concerns with the bank/trustee. The beneficiary should keep in mind that he has the right to change the

This working article is hosted by Law Mexico Publishing and may not be commercially reproduced without the permission of the copyright holder. http://lawmexico.com/publications.htm Copyright 2009 Dennis John Peyton.

bank/trustee if the conditions of the agreement do not meet his satisfaction. Since there are transaction fees that must be paid to carry out the assignment, if a change of bank/trustee is called for this would be the best time to do so. The buyer could save money in extra fees by having several changes made at the same time.

STEP SEVEN: CLOSING AND TITLE TRANSFER

"Closing" is defined as: "1. The act of transferring ownership of a property form seller to buyer in accordance with a sales contract. 2. The time when a closing takes place." In a Mexican real estate transaction, closing takes place at the moment the transaction is recorded before a public notary or public broker. However, although the sales contract is binding for the buyer and the seller, it is not **perfected** until it is filed with the public registry. *Black's Law Dictionary* defines **perfect instrument**: "An instrument is said to become perfect or perfected when recorded (or registered) or filed for record, because it then becomes good as to all the world."

The public notary files the sales contract, trust agreement, etc. with the public registry shortly after he has recorded it. The buyer will receive a certified copy of the contract just as soon as it has been filed. Proof of filing is normally on one of the last pages of the recorded contract in the form of a stamp giving the time and date it was filed.

The **closing date**, or the date on which the seller delivers the deed and the buyer pays for the property, is the date the contract is recorded by the notary. As far as the buyer and seller are concerned, the transaction is closed at the moment the contract is executed before the notary, so the sales price is paid at this time. The notarized contract is a public instrument and as such cannot be unilaterally reversed by any of the parties. This is why most transactions are closed at this stage.

In transactions involving trust agreements the bank/trustee usually acts on behalf of the buyer when it comes to closing. For this reason, the buyer's signature is not legally required and he will not necessarily appear before a public notary. However, more and more the banks are requiring beneficiary/buyers to appear and sign at closing. This seems to be to protect the bank but it is not clear just what protection they would actually be afforded. It is best not to release any funds until it is certain that the seller has actually executed the sales contract. Often the seller will execute the agreement in the presence of the notary before the bank does. This is not a problem as long as the bank also executes within the term set by the notary. The buyer should arrange with the bank/trustee and/or the notary to be notified once the seller executes the sale contract. The buyer then can pay the purchase price knowing that the seller cannot back out of the transaction.

TAXES, FEES, AND CLOSING COSTS

There are two taxes that are applied to real estate transactions:

1. The income tax generated from the sale of the property; and,

2. The property acquisition tax.

When the title documents are executed with a public notary, all taxes arising from the transaction must be paid, as well as the notary fees. As a general rule, the seller pays the capital gains tax and the buyer pays the acquisition tax. Although it is possible to negotiate that the seller pay half of any other fee or expense, such as notary fees and the like, if it is a seller's market, the seller inevitably refuses to pay anything more than the capital gains tax.

This working article is hosted by Law Mexico Publishing and may not be commercially reproduced without the permission of the copyright holder. http://lawmexico.com/publications.htm Copyright 2009 Dennis John Peyton.

Closing costs vary widely and are determined by the type of transaction being carried out. The following table is helpful in determining the approximate amount in each case and who is responsible for paying it.

ALL REAL ESTATE TRANSACTIONS:

Concept	Amount	Who Pays
Certificates of no encumbrances and no tax lien	$200 - $300	Negotiable
Notary fees	$750 - $1200	Buyer
Filing fee - Public Registry	$100 to $300	Buyer
Appraisal fee	$300 to $500	Negotiable
Acquisition tax	2% of sales price	Buyer
Income tax	34% of the gain or 20% of sales price	Seller
Attorney's fees	Negotiable	Each pays his own attorney

ADDITIONAL FEES FOR REAL ESTATE TRUSTS

CONCEPT	AMOUNT	WHO PAYS
Bank/Trustee acceptance fee	$350 to $750 flat fee or same as annual fee	Buyer
Bank/Trustee annual fee	1% to 0.20% per annum of the value of the property held in trust, or a minimum of $300 - $3,300	Buyer
Trust permit fee	50 years – approx. $1,00.00	Buyer
Foreign investment registration	$300 - $400-$800	Buyer

STEP EIGHT: FEDERAL CONCESSIONS

THE FEDERAL ZONE

The most common concession is the federal zone concession. A buyer need only concern himself with this concession if purchasing beachfront property. For more information on the federal zone see Chapter Three. A federal concession can only be applied for once the applicant acquires trust rights to the property adjoining the federal zone.

This working article is hosted by Law Mexico Publishing and may not be commercially reproduced without the permission of the copyright holder. http://lawmexico.com/publications.htm Copyright 2009 Dennis John Peyton.

A federal zone concession costs relatively little so acquiring one is advisable once a buyer has completed the steps in the preceding sections. It is not a requirement. The advantage in having the federal zone concession is that it allows the concessionaire to build or make improvements in the federal zone and, maybe more importantly, it eliminates the possibility of someone else getting the concession for that area. It is unlikely that a concession will be granted to someone other than the owners of the property adjoining the federal zone, but it is possible.

If a buyer purchases property already held in trust and the beneficiary has the federal zone concession, the buyer needs to contact SEDESOL to have the concession put in his name. The assignment of concession rights must be approved by SEDESOL in order to be valid. A buyer cannot assume that because he purchases beachfront property he is automatically entitled to the concession held by the former trust beneficiary.

All applications involving foreigners are subject to special procedures and the opinion of the General Direction of the Federal Real Estate (*Dirección General del Patrimonio Inmobiliario Federal*). An application for a federal zone concession is submitted before the local office of the Secretary of Social Development (*Secretaria de desarrollo social*) otherwise known as SEDESOL.

Some or all of the following information is submitted depending on the property and the kind and location of improvements.

APPLICATION

The application is presented in triplicate, in writing, signed by the applicant or by his legal representative, and must contain the following:

1. Applicant's name. In the case of a corporation or legal entity, the trade name or corporate name.

2. Domicile and address at which to receive notifications.

3. Exact location of the area being applied for, indicating state, municipality, colony, town, housing subdivision and name of the place.

4. Indication of the total surface needed for the concession.

5. Description of the area for concession, according to its legal nature as follows: a) Federal Maritime Terrestrial Zone; b) Lands Gained From the Sea; c) Lands Gained From Any Other Maritime Water Tanks.

6. Detailed description of the metes and bounds of the total surface.

7. Description of the use, exploitation and/or improvement of the federal area.

8. For the exploitation of materials, a description of its use and precedence, as well as its characteristics, extraction volume and commercial value (where the material is obtained from, its characteristics, quantity of extraction, calculate the volume of stratum and existing deposits that are intended for the extraction and the commercial value consistent with the local current markets).

9. Applicant's legal capacity with regard to the property adjacent to the federal zone applied for, and a determination of the relationship as follows: Owner; *Ejidatario*; Joint Tenant; Possessor; Usufructuary; Tenant; Others.

10. Explanation that the use claimed for the federal area is congruent with the corresponding Urban Development Plans authorized for that zone. (Federal, State and/or Municipality).

This working article is hosted by Law Mexico Publishing and may not be commercially reproduced without the permission of the copyright holder. http://lawmexico.com/publications.htm Copyright 2009 Dennis John Peyton.

11. Indication of any installations or improvements in the area where applicant is applying for concession; if so, an indication of their characteristics and estimated value.

12. Term requested for the concession.

13. Amount of the total investment.

14. If the adjacent property is intended to be integrated with the federal zone, the application should contain an indication of the following: a) The use, exploitation or improvements of both; b) The type of work/construction projected to be done in both. c) The amount to be invested in both.

15. Description of the installations to be carried out in the federal zone, indicating the different stages to be taken for the execution of the project.

16. Depending upon the magnitude of projects and investments to be executed, SEDESOL will require the applicant to amplify its application, explain, or add more elements to it, to better understand, according to the policy of this agency.

17. For the investments referred to above, or depending on the use or exploitation of the federal land applied for in the concession, the applicant should determine if it causes a negative ecological impact in that area.

18. Declaration stating whether the applicant has had other concessions in the federal maritime terrestrial zone or in lands gained from the sea, and, as the case may be, providing all necessary information to identify such concessions.

The following documents should also be presented in triplicate, together with the concession application:

➢ **To accredit applicant's legal status: a) Individuals:** certified copy of applicant's birth certificate, and, if applicable, a naturalization letter. b) **Legal entity or Corporation:** certified copy of the Articles of Incorporation, if applicable, power of attorney granted to the applicant stating that he has legal capacity to act as a legal representative of said corporation. c) Documents stating legal and financial status of the corporation.

➢ **To accredit applicant's legal status in regard to the adjoining property**: a) Certified copy of the property deed, trust, or like legal document. b) Document stating applicant's legal capacity in relation to the property abutting the federal zone (Tenant, Possessor, Usufructuary, etc.).

➢ **Technical Requirements**: a) A plot map giving graphical statistics of the delimitation of the federal maritime terrestrial zone or, in its case, delimitation of the lands gained from the sea, which should be approved by SEDESOL and by the federal zone agency that corresponds to the property. b) A survey map of the projects, legally approved by the corresponding authorities, as well as a description of said projects. c) A programmed schedule of the investments and projects execution. d) Eight photographs of the area the applicant is applying for, taken from the ocean to the land, from the most important spots and from the different cardinal points if possible.

➢ **Additional Documentation**: a) A favorable ecological impact report issued from SEDESOL if applicable. b) Appraisal for revenues on the existing construction, said appraisal shall be issued by the National Real Estate Appraisal Commission. c) Any other technical, administrative and legal documents that the Secretariat may require to fulfill this application.

This working article is hosted by Law Mexico Publishing and may not be commercially reproduced without the permission of the copyright holder. http://lawmexico.com/publications.htm Copyright 2009 Dennis John Peyton.

EXTENSION OF APPLICATIONS

Any concessionaire, who wishes to extend his concession, should apply for an extension at least 30 natural days before the concession's expiration date. If he doesn't comply, the rights he holds will expire.

The Extension Application should contain the following:

➤ File number and Concession date.
➤ All the requirements mentioned in number 1, 2, 3 and 12 of the Application section above.
➤ Verification or rectification, as the case may be, the use, exploitation or improvements made regarding the public property in question, as well as the total surface area requested.
➤ Any improvements or installation affected by the concession, according to the original concession, should be listed with a description and estimated value. This is necessary because upon the termination of the concession such improvements will become property of the Federal Government.
➤ An express statement that the concessionaire agrees to cover the fees related to the use, enjoyment and exploitation of the federal zone as well as any other improvements.
➤ If there is a project for a new construction, as well as any additions, modifications, or demolition, the above information should be submitted in order to obtain an authorization from SEDESOL.
➤ The amount to be invested and schedule of execution.
➤ Appraisal for revenues on the existing construction issued by the National Real Estate Appraisal Commission (*Commisión de Avalúos de Bienes Nacionales).*

This working article is hosted by Law Mexico Publishing and may not be commercially reproduced without the permission of the copyright holder. http://lawmexico.com/publications.htm Copyright 2009 Dennis John Peyton.